All the Way to China

poems by

Maria Rouphail

Finishing Line Press
Georgetown, Kentucky

All the Way to China

Publisher: Leah Huete de Maines
Editor: Christen Kincaid
Cover Art: Paul Rouphail
Author Photo: Maria Rouphail
Cover Design: Paul Rouphail

Order online: www.finishinglinepress.com
also available on amazon.com

Author inquiries and mail orders:
Finishing Line Press
P. O. Box 1626
Georgetown, Kentucky 40324
U. S. A.

Table of Contents

for Asher Michel Rouphail
b. November 24, 2020
A light in the darkness...

. . . and for all my beloveds,
everyone who is, was, and will be
in the world

What is it then between us?
What is the count of the scores or hundreds of years between us?
(Walt Whitman, "Crossing Brooklyn Ferry")

...they dwell in us, waiting for a fulfillment
(Czeslaw Milosz, "Late Ripeness')

Childhood is everything
(Shelby Stevenson, North Carolina Poet Laureate Emeritus
April 8, 2022)

You are my blue Italian skies
(Margie, to her daughters, found among her effects)

The farther away, the better you remember
(mgr, 2022)

I.

All the Way to China

From the hardpan of the New Jersey backyard,
a toy shovel in my four-year-old hand,
and Mama saying,
Go on dig deep dig all the way to China,
it comes to this: a desk, a chair,
and an immense window holding
a white granite sky, pearl sun, a bridge's silver scarp.
And a dark river hauling out of a glacier in Tibet,
all dragon sheen and muscle moving
through this city on the other side of the world.

(Nanjing, Peoples' Republic of China, 2019)

The Origin of Poetry

my body played back
what it recorded
it didn't explain
for the longest time
I didn't know why
I heard blood pound
in the summer thunderclap
the repairman's hammer
the knocking of water pipes
behind plaster walls

my heart raced
at the sounds I heard inside me
I stood frozen at the door
for revelations
I came into speech
when my body needed words
in the thick of the storm

They All Scattered

Call it Life.
Call it Fate.
Call it the two Great Wars.
Call it shellshock and an uncle,
survivor of trenches,
rocking back and forth
on the front stoop all day.
You don't have to be dead to be gone—
Call it a paterfamilias
trying to murder his wife with a plumber's chain.
Gray-eyed Margie, the oldest, fought him off.

Call it the Great Depression,
the Great American Century.
Say it was that same father, then the mother dying.
A boy with a killer heart that did him in
before he turned thirty.
His kid brother worked on bombers
in the North African desert.
After FDR, after D-Day,
Margie's people picked up, headed west or south—
across the Hudson, down the Jersey coast.
Florida, New Mexico, California.
Maybe only two counties to the east,
far as they could.

You knew them, or you heard what they did.
You imagine how it must have been,
though you are no closer to understanding
than if they had been Pleistocenes
with flint knives and hand axes.
Call what you're about
the prising open of locks, the laying of wreaths—
these presumptions and poems.
This work you need to do.

Gray-Eyed Bronx Girl

(Margie, 1915)

Sliding between your mother's thighs
at four minutes past ten on the thirteenth of August,
a Friday night in a year of the War to End All Wars,
you were scarcely more
than baby bone and newborn hair.

But how your father railed at your mother
for not holding you in until after midnight.

Bad luck to be born on Friday the thirteenth,
as if the madness from his mouth
could do a thing about it.
Not even your cries moved him.

Someone washed and swaddled you,
and he looked away.
Even later, after sons came, your brothers,
he looked away.

Gray-eyed girl,
when you took your first
breath in that Bronx apartment,
the smell of fried meat and bootleg lay
like a greasy sheet on your birthing bed.
You were already on the way to becoming
your mother's hiding place, a little drawer of secrets.

Did you dream you'd birth a baby girl,
that one day I'd day sing our survival song?

Before Words, the Body's Inscription (1948)

Do you remember when you were in her belly?
(MG, aged 5, to her sister who writes poems)

Even before she is pregnant, it's said
Margie is tormented, scalded by sorrow.
Foreboding and dread are her food.
Thus at my beginning I hear
her heart's blood-surge, the turbulence
of her morning sickness and the weeping.

Her body is a noisy cistern
grinding, whooshing, gurgling.
Sounds seep into the amniotic sac.
My embryonic cochleae vibrate to the tumult.

In due time, I outgrow my cave and begin to free myself.
But Margie listens to a tyrannical nurse
who chastises her for not working hard enough to push me out.
She seizes up, fears she's doing it all wrong,
which is when I stop moving.

The doctor, a confident man known to eat an apple in one hand
while holding a crowning infant's head in the other,
extracts me with forceps.
I am pulled into the world
through a sluice of water and placental blood.
I am at once the object of hands that wash me,
and tongues that bless the light at my birth.

But my body will remember.
For a long time, it will not know why.
It will hear the scolding voice and pounding blood
in the summer thunderclap,
the repair man's hammer,
the knocking of water pipes behind plaster walls.
My heart will race at the sounds.
I will stand frozen at the door.

Mother and Daughter, Two Voices

I.

Daughter

Some days you sat yourself down   on a straight back chair at the kitchen
table   and rested your head in your hand   Your gray eyes got quiet and
steady   Your lips parted slightly like you wanted   to talk to somebody
only you could see   and I tried to climb onto your lap   *What's wrong
Mama What's wrong?*   And you said *Nothing! Go and play!*   Even
though I knew different   even though I tried to get you to tell me   what
made you look that way   you only said *Nothing! Go and play!*

You prayed novenas   Lit candles before an icon   And when the spark of
me took hold   you marked a calendar for each day of the months I lived
inside you   Marked the day when I first turned   Marked the day when
you first felt me kick   Marked the hour when you started to squeeze me
out Even later   when you pulled me by the hair to the kitchen sink and
held my throat against cold porcelain   Even when you chunked bars of
Ivory soap into my mouth   because I'd done something bad   Even then,
I could not say   you did not love me.

Heading West

In your whole life you flew only once.
It was night, and the need was urgent.
Wordless the whole way, you clenched my hand.
Not just the funeral, you later said, but the flying
made you dig crescent moons into my palm.

It was my first flight, too,
and I turned from your closed face to the soft
curve of the semi-lit window and watched
streetlights rivering under the belly and wing.
I was so young, wanting to believe
the future waited *out there* in the blue-violet night.

Tonight, I'm on a jetliner heading west,
descending through thirty thousand feet,
four decades to the hour when you whispered
death was like diving in an airplane.
Your lungs rose and fell for the last time.

Right now an orange sky bends over LA,
freeways writhe like ropes of fire.
The ocean is a thick black rim.
Sometimes I miss you past all telling.

How my mind is

like the baby grand piano in the front   room of the house on North Taylor Avenue.   The very one I saw in the glossy ads   and purchased off the showroom floor   right out of the shipping crate.   I wanted out-of-the-box perfection   finest steel, wood, and gleaming layers of black lacquer. But, no, *this one*   broken in the upper octaves (I discovered after the fact) thrashes on layers of green felt   like dinner plates in the cupboard   when the commuter locomotives on the double tracks   near the house throttle up their diesel engines.   The piano tuner says   not a thing can be done for it.   To rattle is as much in the nature of this singular instrument   as holds true of china in the swill of train noise.   An intractable situation when hammers hit wires in the high registers.   Oh sure, I can trick my ear to hear notes that sound on key.   But there is always the ring of something hard. No matter how I tune it.   No matter how I play.

Prayer

You could stop on your way to the world's mayhem,
even as the supplications of the ages oppress your heart.

You could come here, rest on my porch.
I wouldn't ask you for a thing. Not one miracle.

Neither wheedling by me, nor bargains struck.
Nothing sworn or forsworn. Your own self alone,

silent or singing, is sweetness sufficient to save
me from crying out loud in the place I've come to—

this painted sky, these faux clouds and the horizon too close,
in this country of nightmares.

Let the mad and the malevolent rage.
I'll fix us supper, and we'll take our ease.

And you could talk to me of your rescues,
of violated bodies and faith betrayed,

cities and coastlines aflame with war, burning trees
the melting ice caps.   And your notorious mercy

people say seeps like rain into the hardened human crust.
How you show the way of wakefulness, endurance—

I will listen carefully for lessons.
Then, when you are rested and rise from the table

with its empty glasses, plates, and rumpled napkins,
I will fold your hands in mine, and being bold

I will kiss you and thank you for coming,
thank you, thank you with all my heart.

And you could go on then, to wherever you were heading
before I hailed you from the porch and asked you to sit a while.

II.

Holiday Outing

1.

This rented chassis tricked out in the latest luxuries. You climb into the back row. It's your ride into town this winter night, and you're packing in with family you've gained through the marriage of one of your children, en route to a waterfront celebration you wouldn't miss for the world. You're not used to such opulence. The whisper doors, the cockpit loaded with apps for data and entertainment, the onboard television, a woman's Chardonnay voice decanting from a speaker. *Fasten your seat belt.* The irony is not lost on you of the chromium badge soldered onto the rear hatch, signifying the make of this vehicle named for a president born into penury in a Kentucky cabin. This rubs you like jagged metal. You don't know why a spasm rises in your throat. It feels like a sob.

My Dead, You Cannot Visit Them

Consider where they lie, here and there.
In a vast meadow abutting a municipal airport.
Among weeds in a potter's field.
Unmarked on a trash-strewn hill near an urban expressway.
Immured with strangers who fought in a war.

My dead.
You cannot visit them.
Scattered while they were in the flesh,
so are they now in the earth.
One never knew them apart from being their child,
or *their* having been someone's children with not enough to eat,
with their endangered bones bowed or broken in so many places.

I always wanted to do some compensatory thing,
to right the scales powerful thumbs had tipped.
I wandered distant homelands where I stood in rivers of wind,
listening for voices. I am listening, still.

My dead, you cannot visit them. Not now.
They were not the kind who lived in one place long enough
to bestow a name on fields, bridges, and boulevards.
For the others, the illustrious ones, alabaster angels stand guard
at the doors of mossy marble vaults under massive oak canopies.

Not like my dead,
pieces of paper in a little cedar box.

Woman on a Plane

"and it shook [her] heart to the very bottom"
Goli Taragui

1

The widow expired in the economy cabin. At a staggering height, somewhere between Boston and London, she leaned against the dark window and died.

She'd been accustomed to exile and passport checkpoints. For years her children shuttled her from one city to another. Whenever their lives overwhelmed, which was often, they dispatched her to one or the other sibling, sending their mother into the sky like smoke from a burning rubbish pile. *You know how much you love it there,* they'd coax. *Besides, you could use a change of scenery.*

Her several grandchildren on various continents spoke only the languages of their parents' new countries. She understood nothing, which made her weep. So, on this flight, when she felt her spirit lifting toward the afterglow of sunset, she told it, *Yes. Go—*

2

Of course, this is a fiction by a writer of considerable repute. But there is another woman, real enough, in a window seat closing a book of short stories on her lap.

She leans into the plexiglas above a wing and looks out at fields stitched with rivers and wisps of snow-flecked uplands. From this height, she sees generations unfolding from her flesh, just as she came forth from couplings no one remembers.

She likes the idea of her sons and daughters-in-law gathered at the airport to receive her. This makes the blood knock in her temples.

We are known in a parcel of light passing swiftly through the world. That's what she'll tell them. Now her heart is beating like a wing. She looks again at the earth, straining to see desert flowers fluttering in her wake.

Marianne

In her parents' country, she was Mirjana,
only child of a widow who survived the war in Europe.
Her father had died violently, on an unlit street—
It was dark, she said. Perhaps this was in the capital,
during the uprising in the year we were born.
Perhaps his wife was pregnant,
and he'd never met his daughter.
She rarely mentioned him.
I live here now, she told me.

We were in the seventh grade.
I watched her—solitary, like me,
slender as a sea oat stalk,
hunched over her desk at the back of the classroom,
all knuckles and wrist bones,
writing, writing, writing —
When I told her that I, too, I had notebooks
where I wrote—*poems,* I said—
she showed me her stories
and sketches of horses.

Once, I walked with her
to a duplex apartment building
where she and her mother lived,
a few blocks from the bridge to the barrier island
and the beach hotels and tourist bars.
She let herself in every afternoon,
started her homework or did some laundry,
waiting for her mother to come home
from the day-shift cleaning hotel rooms.

What I remember
is the chime of a wall clock,
the kitchen that smelled of apples
and the little round table,
our books in a tumble on the faded
red Formica and Marianne reading aloud

her story of a colt separated from its dam and sire,
roaming alone among rocks in a moonless wasteland.
I didn't understand.
A horse might stumble in a place like that, she said over her shoulder,
as she poured Coca Cola into two juice glasses.
Its fetlocks are fragile. And if it fractured a leg—
Her voice trailed off.

I remember the colored pencil drawing
of a flaxen-maned palomino filly—unmistakable,
the resemblance to its creator!—dish-faced, with dark
eyes flashing, slender hooves cantering on the blue
lines of notebook paper ripped from its wire coil.

Portrait of My Cuban Father on His Birthday

(New York City, ca. 1940)

If sorrow—and surely there had been sorrow—
yet, not now in the irises cast slightly
askance in the camera's exploding light,
nor on the full lips, tongue-tipped moist and closed.

Here on the linen-finish page,
the young bachelor in black and white,
broad and clean-shaven under thick brows.

Time was when naked feet and too-small britches said
You will never see adulthood—

But that was in the cyclone years, and he was
el Huracán, indigent rain child, a black-eyed
squall of hunger and orphaned infant flesh.

Call him a grown man now, a triumph
of eye and mouth, tie and fedora, silk and wool.
Vindication on this dress-up day.

In the Faded Photo, My Toddler Self at the Bronx Zoo

doing what every not-yet-two–year-old does:
learning the world by eating it, one lick at a time.

My tongue was the teacher in the schoolroom of my mouth,
and this day's lesson was the finial of a handrail, its feel and taste.

In the photo, a hand pulls me away.
Or have I eluded its grip?

Irresistible iron-flavored globe on my tongue!
Sun-warmed element wrung from a mountain in Pennsylvania,

and polished to perfection in New York!
Fire and earth mixed with my mouth's juices.

On a spring afternoon, incarnate
light and heat spilled over my lips.

What I Learned in the Dark, Under the Covers

(for Margie)

                    In the side yard you saw me
snatch a sharp and shiny thing from my sister's hand.
A ribbon of her blood curled in the water of the little pool.

                              Naturally,
you ran to scoop up your baby girl, away from me,
and soothe her wailing.

            You stripped me of tee shirt and shorts,
clapped me under the covers of my bed,
so I could consider my crime.
I sobbed like any child, striving through gulps
of snot and air to shape the words,
                              I don't know . . .

I was just shy of five,
but when you drew the blinds and shut the door,
I knew something dark snaked from me, too.

                    I could not explain the *why* of it.

Did I tell you I wanted to disappear? Go away
in Papa's blue Ford if that would make things right?
Woe wedged in like the edge of an axe.

Then, in the dark of that room, something rose—

                              a pure presence,

as if the sun had risen on the first day of the world,
and I was the clear sky.

                    The *I am* in me
refused to pass into nothingness.

Wonder Woman

That's me, taken by Margie, my mother,
with a Brownie camera on black and white
film she bought at the Walgreen's in those days.

Snapped me in a homemade costume sometime
around the first of November, Feast of All Saints.
Me, as the Blessed Virgin Mary,

posing in front of our cinderblock duplex
with its jalousie windows. You can see the double rows
of aluminum-clad panes rolled open slightly,

just over my shoulders, the way they made them back then.
And the stucco siding, washed out and mildewed
by seasons of subtropical rain.

No matter. I am the Mother of Jesus in her glory.
You can tell by the photo that Mama has
sewn me a white veil and tunic. But my cloak is pale blue,

Mary's color, for the children's Mass and school party.
The Sisters have told us to come as our patron saints
and since Mary is one of my names, her task is easy.

I ask her, *please* make me look just like the statue in church,
with my brown hair parted down the middle
and my blue mantel flowing over my outstretched arms

like rivers of holiness. I want you to think of clouds parting,
and the winged heads of bodiless cherubs, a twilit Milky Way,
golden shafts of grace shooting down to the earth from Mary's palms.

So what if Mama has bobby-pinned my veil to my fly-away bangs,
and my ankle socks and saddle shoes are showing below the hem?
I'll just kick them off, let the stiff grass scratch my ankles and toes.

Look close, and see the Queen of Heaven and Earth.
Queen of the whole cosmic shebang, in fact,
its quarks and neutrinos, black holes and dark matter.

I am the New Eve crowned with supernovae,
standing on the north pole of a minor planet,
crushing a snake with my bare feet.

The Amazing Nowness of Then

Could be that slap on the jaw so hard your four-
year-old brain sloshed in your skull. Maybe the
bar of Ivory soap crammed into your mouth, the
alkaline flecks of rendered fat that coated the
cusps of your milk teeth and made you gag.
Maybe it was your hair roots ringing with pain,
the belt buckle across your bare legs for god-
knows-what unforgettable lesson you needed to
learn. And the incisions their tongues made
when they teased you about your vomit-stained
hospital sheets, the reek of your little body so
bad it made the nurse retch.

What you thought you'd buried in the cold
ground and walked away from, and the memory
no more than a line of pale keloid on your belly.
Then someone turns to you and says something
about nothing. Nothing at all.
And suddenly you're stopped in your tracks,
swept back to your kindergarten scars, your
soiled bed, the middle-of-the night petitions to
God, the pile of dirt you never stopped being.

And for the life of you,
you can't figure out why you end up in the very
place where you had to keep your eyes and ears
open all the time.
Why you haven't gotten over it.
Because isn't that
what you're supposed to damn well do
when you grow up,
take yourself in hand?

No, seriously—

Annotated

Shut up
or I'll give you
something to cry about!
Filthy thing, you!
When are you going to learn?
Why can't you follow directions?
Who do you think you are?
Who gave you permission?
Who died and left you boss?
Little brat!
Pain in the ass!
Rotten kid!
You should have seen yourself!

Why are you crying?
Why can't you take a joke?
Why are you so difficult?
Why is everything a big deal?
Why are you so sensitive?
Why are you always like this?
Why can't you get over it?
Why are you so crazy
Why are you such a bitch?

Aren't you past an age to obsess
about what happened
long ago?
Aren't you making your life
more difficult than it needs to be?
Can't you just let it go?
Can't you just shake it off?
Look in the mirror, say to yourself,

I'm OK.

Purification

Mama scrubs the dirty sheets
Mama scrubs the toilet seats
Mama scrubs the dirty floors
Mama scrubs the dresser drawers

And when you told, almost seventy years after,
about your mother dragging you by the hair to the kitchen sink
and her fist shoving the bar of soap into your four-year-old mouth,
all because you'd licked a sick girl's lollipop,
your friend looked up from her latte and leaning in said,
I believe she was trying to purify you.

And when you considered for some hours,
the baby bibs your mother bleached day after day, and the bed
linens whipping and snapping on the clothesline,
and the little girls' underpants, the ladies' bra, and Papa's boxer
shorts wrung hard with her bare hands, how she curved her back
and shoulders over the tub (or hunched her hip against the kitchen sink)
and twisted the cotton bath towels and flannel pajamas like screws,
then pinned them to the rope that sagged in the January wind—

remembering, too, your First Communion day (as if you could ever forget)
and the spring cloudburst and gusts of wind, your tulle veil in the plastic
bag flying out the window of the blue Ford into the rushing river of mud,
and your mother jumping from the passenger seat to pluck it from the flood—
how she dirtied her own hands to save it from the storm sewer,
then held it before the O's of your wide eyes and mouth,
the dripping bag with the spotless veil, saying
This veil is YOU, and this filth is the world
from which she was hell-bent on preserving her child.

You can see now, as clear as a cloudless day
the sign of your unsullied self she offered
from her soap-cracked hands with dried blood in the knuckle folds.
Like the body of Christ you received on your tongue that morning
from the hands of the priest.

And though it has taken so long, you know at last
this was the way she loved you, the way she wanted you to stay.
Pure as Jesus. How else can you explain it?

Word of the Lord

The word of the Lord came to me, saying
Who can bear to hear any more about that soap thing,
or the blue Ford and your First Communion veil—

The word of the Lord came to me, saying
What are you writing over and over?
People will think you're obsessed. Besides, after you're gone,
no one will read your poems—

The word of the Lord came to me, saying
BTW and FYI, she wasn't as crazy as you make her out.
She had her reasons, as well I know.
You could try being more fair—

I answered and said to the Lord
But I, too, have reasons. As well you know.
My body and mind, the tablet
on which these words are chiseled—
it's the text I have.

III.

Holiday Outing

2.

So you buckle up and close your eyes. You cock your head to one side, nestling it against a window. You give your body to the heated leather that cradles your back. And you expand in this warmth, as you did on summer days when your mother sat you in the rear seat of the blue Ford for the ride to the beach, your father driving with the windows open, and her kerchief *snap-snapping* in the wind.   And now you make space for the ongoing conversation up front. The thirty-year-old in-law who is the volunteer chauffeur tonight, talking about a marathon he's training for, the people he knows about, famous for running in this part of the country. You can hear how much he wants this. How hard he's working. A woman's voice intersects his, something about what *she* did decades ago to run in that very race. Something about breathing. Something about patience. Lots of it. *Oh, yeah,* he'll do fine, just fine. Laughter now.   Voices circle, touch, trail away like wisps of a campfire.

First Memory

I asked a friend, What is the earliest memory of your childhood? She said it was a clear winter day in the city. Said she was dressed in a flamingo pink snowsuit with appliqued flowers. She wore little white boots. Her mother and her aunt held each hand as she toddled down the sidewalk. She asked me, What is the earliest memory of your childhood? I said, I was in my highchair in the kitchen. My mother put a powdered sugar donut on the tray, which I promptly picked up and threw to the floor. I remember wanting to do this. I clearly remember wondering, *Is this arm mine? Does this hand belong to me?* I liked the pasty ooze on my fingers squishing the greasy donut, the act of tossing it without a notion of why, the little puff of sugar smoke when it hit the floor. I remember the soft sound of the donut exploding on the tiles, little pieces of pastry breaking away. I remember it was my left hand that did the throwing. It was the hand that eventually learned to write. I remember my mother laughed.

Annunciation

(after Lynn Emmanuel)

for Robert

He wants to be born.
So first he enters the dream of the woman
a doctor has told will never conceive.

He lets himself in through the gate
of her sleeping brain during a hard snow
in late November.

He gives himself eyes and hair like hers,
wraps himself in thick fleece, his fingers curving
over the hem, like the paws of a burrowing mammal.

She wakes with the dream of him still clinging,
*I've birthed a black-eyed baby boy, I've carried him
up the aisle of the church to the baptismal font.*

She goes to the window where slantwise
snow erases the houses across the street.
Only a curbside lamp on its iron stalk breaks through,
          a yellow clot in the boreal blur.

After she has laid aside the dream or forgotten it,
he enters her body sometime in January.
His arrival ignites engines and fires up turbines

with power unknown to her, making her whole
being a construction zone for the laying of foundations,
the framing of the many rooms of his evolving body.

In April, cornerstone and beam well set and level,
he shows her his brain and spine, a string of perfect lights
blinking in the midnight sky of the sonogram.

The doctor is speechless. But the woman
rehearses the names of her beloved living and dead.
She will pick one of them.

She watches the tiny heart strobe in its cage.
Beacon of what is coming in October.
A swaddling blanket. A christening.

What the Midwife Said

"She picks her way through the snow like a tightrope walker,
supervising each step on sidewalk ice. She sends one arm

out from the waist, a stave against falling, and folds the other
over her belly in a winter coat each month more taut.

She catches me watching her push her way to the L,
and she waves across a snowbank. I smile and wave back.

My neighbor, this woman well past youth,
filling up with her first child.

I've told her about my sons and daughters, all grown.
Like her, I was having babies past thirty-five,

two in an Illinois blizzard.

Forty years a midwife, and my eye is still sharp.
My hands know just where to glide along the flanks

from pubis to fundus to find a baby's lie,
its head and breech, size and weight.

I'll be there for her, my neighbor,
when high waves of pain roll

and the child churns like a Great Lakes prow in winter,
breaking through the strait of blood and water,

sliding into blue air, white light."

The Music Box

A little bear is beating a soldier boy's drum.

    Oh, Mama, I'm weeping

I'm weeping and I can't tell why.

A hard snow is falling and the baby
I'm feeding at my breast is sleeping

    he's sleeping

His fluttering lids are closing
as the treacle tune plays

    toy land, toy land . . .

His lips are now unpursed and parted,
his pretty, milky dream has started
far from the December dark ticking toward night,

and the moonless pane returns my face
in the slant lamp light.

    Oh, Mama!

I'm turning the key again to hear the tune play
for me, you know, for me.

My Not-Baby

(after Lucille Clifton)

for your wet ripeness in my pouch of unripe eggs,
your burst from it and then
the float into the dark juices of the strait,
for your half-self melting
with your half-self swimming toward you,
your whole new being becoming more,
for the not-shelter of my womb,
the failure of the luxurious blanket of my blood,
for the unplanting of the placenta
or the never-planting—
for not knowing, not knowing
until spasms and the flood washed you from me,
and you were not anymore—
for you, my not-child
this too-late letter, this sorrow-song.

Margie Skips a Grade

Imagine a sallow girl, tall for her age and quiet,
in a Bronx classroom with high double-hung windows
and looming pendulum lights.
Imagine that girl with her chin in her hand
while her classmates stumble over ai, ia, ie, ei,
and the multiplication tables, and those long division problems
she'd conquered in no time flat.
Imagine Mrs Levy writing her parents a note
in the midterm report card about their very bright daughter,
accomplished in every subject beyond any of her peers.
She's headed to college, Mrs Levy predicts in her beautiful hand,
no question about it.

Imagine the girl six, maybe seven years later telling herself,
Yes.
I will go to the University.
I will become an anthropologist.
I will live in India.
I will write . . .
Imagine her saying this out loud one night
as she and her mother wash the dishes.
The mother turns to the girl and shaking her head
slowly, slowly, says: *There's no money. There's hardly enough food.*

For the sake of the little ones, the girl will go to work.
Woolworth's, at first. A counter girl.

Imagine her standing at that greasy sink in 1930,
passing the dripping plates to her mother, one by one,
remembering Mrs Levy. And that once-girl
who had been so bright she'd skipped a grade.
Imagine her at recess, with friends swarming in wonder,
their hands touching her face, her hair, her arms.
Oh, Margie! Oh, Margie!

Still Life: an Aftermath

(for Margie, who had to move far away from the place that had lifted
her heart and made it glad)

Broken,
but not quite like a mirror
or a china cup.

Fractured,
but not as a bone cracks,
or a tooth.

Shattered, yes, but
more like *split open* with
sudden violence,

a swift sundering,
as houses sink
into a gaping seam

and are no more.

Whether
as in an earthquake, or a *just as*
rupture of some similitude:

a rending all the same, with
the already-begun pain you knew
was coming.

Margie's Daughters Wait for Her to Pick Them Up from School

(Miami, 1956)

We chase each other around
the big banyan tree in the parking lot.
My sister says the fat roots look like old people's feet.
Like Mama's feet, though she's not old.

My sister and I run and run. We overheat
in our uniforms, pale green with creamy
white stripes, like the big vines
winding up the trunk of a nearby palm.
We throw our book bags down, trouncing
the banyan tree's hammer toes until our ankles hurt.
Our mouths turn all cottony with thirst.
Our midriffs begin to soak with sweat.

Mama said to wait at the tree, wait for her
to drive up in the secondhand De Soto coupe
Papa bought when she cried so hard
about her mother dying, and missing Aunt Sis.
How she wanted us to go back north,
how she said we would do it someday.

The last bell rang a long time ago, and now
the parking lot is almost empty.
Besides us, the only one around is a skinny red-haired
boy with a limp. He's swooped away in a blue and white
sedan, past some eighth-grade girls
twittering down the road like squirrels.

We're alone now. My sister scooches down
between the knobby knuckles of the banyan tree.
I stay on my feet, bracing one hand against the trunk,
squinting into the horizon for a sign of the car.

She's coming, she is ...
We say this over and over,
trying to keep each other from crying.

Margie Takes a Stand

Can't tell when it came to me
to set out for this new territory.
Every morning I stoop over a basket
of wet underwear and socks. I hang them
under clouds reminding me of fish bones.

But today I've ironed my best dress,
polished my shiny pocketbook and black shoes,
washed my hair and set it in smooth movie star waves.

My daughter at the kitchen table,
hunched over her algebra homework, turns her head
and asks where I am going so dressed up
on this afternoon in the middle of the week.
Shopping, I say.

I make the short drive to the mall
with its archipelago of stores. I stand
before the automatic doors of the A&P.
Shoppers glance at the cardboard sign I've made
with my own hands. It tells them to stop buying grapes.

> *Justice for migrant workers!*

I call to people coming and going.
I'm fearless now, whether or not they listen,
whether or not they care

> *how many have fallen in the fields . . .*

"Neighbors"

(a sonnet sequence, after a painting by Margie's brother, an artist)

Margie's brother presents her with the painting (Miami 1958)

So warm for a winter's day in this city near
the tropic of Capricorn. I've come
all the way from New York (childhood home
where in another age my fear-
less sister and I were born) to pay a debt
incurred in our youth, result of boldness
in the face of a parent's anger. She, the oldest
defied our drunken father and often put
her own body between me (her brother),
and our father's flailing fist. She dreamed
for herself oceans and islands. She framed
for me a future as no other
had. She always said, *You'll be a fine
painter.* To her I bring this work of mine.

Margie hangs the painting on a sunlit wall

Sun in the room makes the dust motes rise,
and a gust from the sea five miles away
lifts the curtain's hem. My full skirt sways
like a royal palm as I hang the surprise
my brother brings. I put it in a bright place
between two chairs covered in coral-colored
cotton. I stand here with the brother I honor
for making it, this long-ago boy whose face
and back our father broke into a hundred blue-
black pieces. After all these years they've not grown
together to make him whole. If stones
in his way did not trip him, in due
time his wounds would heal. Here, the canvas his labors
perfected, an Antillean scene he's titled, *Neighbors*.

While admiring the painting, Margie gazes at her brother

Neighbors with its overlapping
triangles of familiar forms—two coffee-hued
women—one caressing a baby, the other giving food
to a toddler. And a broad-bellied, strapping
man in a white Panama hat. A brown-skinned father
shoeless, upright and calm, towering
over a squinty- eyed girl cowering
beside him. Black-haired Carib child, his daughter
perhaps, a yellow bloom over her right ear, who frowns
(like my child frowns, for no reason I know) as though
she's tamping down tears. My eyes go
to her, then back to the artist's face pitched down,
askance, as though he's listening to something,
or, in this sunlit room, he's dreaming.

Margie's brother, his artist's statement

The painting dreams of getting it right—
mood   color   scene.
When I am not raging, or careen-
ing recklessly down the dark night
of memory, I make good art.
I coax the spirit from my subject.
Not surface, but substance, the correct
aim of portraiture. I find it hard,
unsatisfactory, to work without
living models, whom I sometimes dress in
costumes not theirs, or I change their skin
color, I experiment. Unorthodox, no doubt.
Consider the girl I painted with a frown:
my sister's child who didn't smile until four months grown.

Margie's brother reveals more about the model for the child in the painting

For half a year I worked on this piece.
I shaped the girl's face and hair.
Her hand, as well. Here and there
a trace of pigment to suggest the crease
of her mouth and brow, the yellow flower.
My sister's child craved perfection. She wanted
me to teach her to draw, and was undaunted
except by a fear of failure,
as when her blue crayon slipped
below the lines in the coloring book —
her eyes filled up, but she didn't cry. I took
note of the tremor in her upper lip.
I know about holding back tears. She's a bird
whose song I heard.

Margie foretells her brother's fate

He will crush his own wings, scuttle
his body, toppling from the building where he lives,
I fear that day looms, and it grieves
my heart to know that not all
birds survive the long flight. What good
my brother sees and does despite his pain
will not keep him aloft, and I am powerless. Again
he will plummet, and it would
seem for no reason than he fails
to know his own goodness. What I see
in his painter's skill is the degree
of his yearning to prevail
over pain, the very dream his own life never saw,
figure of himself he could not draw.

What Margie Wrote in *memoriam* about Her Brother

(in her own hand on August 3, 1965)

The bird lay mortally wounded on the city street
His anguished heart now at rest
The frail wings which were bruised so many
       times by life's shackles
Gave mute evidence of the pain they had endured
But the soul was free—wildly soaring toward the heavens
To a rendezvous with those loved ones
       waiting to receive him
Leaving us to wonder where we had failed him
How we could have helped him along this stony path.

Margie's Daughter Talks Back

Wood. Shell. Bone. Buttons
in every size and color your mother saved for mending.

You, too, saved them,
in the round cookie tin on a high shelf.
Rainy days, and you'd take it down
and we'd remember
buttons from faded summer dresses,
buttons from coats returned from war,
buttons with bits of garments still clinging,
flesh and tendon of them. Red grosgrain,
shock of silver wedding silk,
fingers of fragrance still clinging.
Attar of rose and vetiver still clinging.
Heft and pour, the cascading clack and clatter
of buttons, like coins or pretend jewels.

You, too, loved them.
You and I together breathed the old secrets hanging
like the kitchen smells in that Bronx apartment.
Buttons from a man's flannel before zippers were.
Your father's, you said.   And the blue bruise
Your mother tried to hide with a lock of hair when
you, looking, and in your small voice asked,
What happened to your eye, Mama?
as she reattached the right arm of your school sweater.
In the next room the bleats of a baby boy,
and a darkness you hoisted onto your twelve-year-old hip
and hauled through the rest of your life.
Hauled it into my life, too.

Would you believe me if I told you?
I have survived the winter.
Here is the faith I've entered with myself,
rule, rite, and rigor of it:
I will not belong to whatever happens to me.
It's OK to say these things.

Mother and Daughter, Two Voices

II.

Mother

Let me tell you while you can still hear:
the memory of me will be like soap in your mouth
which you will try to spit out.
I will always be the words you taste.
But they will sweeten with time.

Let me tell you while you can still feel:
even when I broke you, you did not break.

Let me tell you so you will believe:
everything you are is sufficient.
You are a river on its way to the sea,
a fire that can't be quenched.

Mother and Daughter, Two Voices

IV.

Holiday Outing

3.

By the time you're halfway to the party on the wharf, you're convinced the people on this ride with you could be in blood and bone your own New York family, driving through the city on a Sunday afternoon in 1954. Talking about someone's niece who broke her engagement and entered a convent in Pennsylvania. Another's cousin married just last month, how his mother would have to live without him so far away in California. How she'd have to take the train, since the plane was so expensive. Maybe the car stopped for a red light, and you watched a round-shouldered bus in the shadow of a cross street load with passengers. Even with the windows up, you smelled the diesel vapors pouring from the exhaust pipe. And you were glad, then, to hunch against a beloved aunt who held forth on Marilyn Monroe and Joe DiMaggio, their whirlwind divorce. You remember sinking into your aunt's voice, dreaming into the sleeve of her coat. And now you're inhaling the smell of the living room closet where she hung her coat all year. Naphthalene. Lily of the valley. How good it felt to be with her, with all of them. How good it feels right now, this very hour, hurtling through the immense black sky.

Dreaming of My Father

It is August fifteenth. We have come to the sea.
You with your work pants rolled up to the knees,
and my obedient feet following you into the surf.
The wind claps my sky-blue skirt to my thighs.

In the dream you tell me the story again
of *La Asunción*, God's mother falling into death's sleep,
her whole self lifting into paradise, and in her honor,
her son breathing a blessing into the sea on every August fifteenth.

Your own mother named you Roberto de la Asunción
before they unclasped your infant hands from her breast
and folded her too-young bones into a pauper's grave.
How could you know you'd never see your island again?

Papa, orphaned daddy, undocumented child riding a ferry
to this cold country that can't tell if it wants people like you,
I still hold the story, hold it like a broken bird in my hands,

In the dream I make my way through waves and wind,
the hem of my skirt floating like a jellyfish.
You turn your face to me and cock your ear
as though, were we patient enough, we'd hear
something from back there—

the roll of African drums.
Chants long, deep, and sweet.
A hymn in Spanish sung by a woman.
A lullaby.

Blue Vase with Dark Foliage

Stop at the glass case,
the ceramic vases for sale,
a suite of them, lapis blue
painted with moss green
leaves and creamy flowers.
Shade gardens in porcelain

> *—morning in early summer, light wind*
> *and a child red-eyed with weeping,*
> *sitting on a blanket under dark trees,*
> *looking up through the leaves …*

Turn the tallest vase in your hand,
finger the smooth dollops of glaze.
What moves in this blueness?

> *—something broken on that picnic day.*
> *Doll or toy. Skin on a knee or elbow …*

You buy the vase because it is beautiful,
like the tree-filled sky and your mother's low voice.

You pack the vase and carry it, a gift to your son's wife.
Somewhere on the way to unwrapping, it is crushed.
The young woman opens the box, catches her breath—

> *It's alright, it's alright,*

she sings, looking up, measuring your face,
taking your hands in hers.

Mother and Son

(after Zbigniew Herbert)

for Paul

From the couch in the living room loud with midday light,

> *How I love your splendid little house on North Third Street—*

I watch you move from cupboard to counter in the open kitchen
where you are preparing us tea

> *the clatter of two spoons on the wood tray*
> *the turn of your wrist as you scoop the leaves into the Turkish pot—*

The volume of Zbigniew Herbert, thick and sleek in its shiny black jacket

> *the one I gave you for your birthday in freshman year*
> *on the flyleaf, "Happy Birthday!" in blue ink—*

I lift it two-handed from the lamp table, flip through and settle randomly
on page two-seventy-four:

"Mother," I begin reading aloud the poet's words, "held onto the beginning of life."
Which is what all mothers do, you know?

> *Boiling water now whistles on the stove.*
> *You cut the flame, then pour the water into the pot—*

That's true, you say, though until the poem Herbert probably never told
how he marveled at that very thing about her, or that the poem itself
was his acknowledgement of the light she'd washed him in all those years

> *you walk the tray into the living room,*
> *setting it down before us—*

She adored him, I reply, despite whatever darkness descended
when he no longer lived nearby or phoned

How could she forget the heat of their bodies when she suckled him,
or his radiant infant beauty?

Maybe he had no more to tell her, you say,
or for love of her, wouldn't. There was the war, after all.
And the end of something.

Hot tea gurgles into white mugs—

Of course, you are right. The young poet decamped, his older self had written,
from the bright city of boyhood.

He'd loosened himself from it—from her—
like a ball of yarn, he said, unwinding into an infinite distance.

the steaming mugs warm the palms of our hands—

Naturally, we agree
he could never return.

Kintsugi

His mama broke him.
That's what the soup kitchen crew say *sotto voce* to me,
the new volunteer, halting their vegetable-chopping
long enough to nod toward the apparition in the doorway.
Broke him to bits from Day One.
I'm thinking this story is one I've heard before: a mother
so broken herself, she knocked chunks of her
child to the floor every chance she had.
Maybe she shook him for being hungry enough to wail through the night.
Maybe she punched him in the stomach after he vomited in his crib.
Broke one of his hands for raiding a bag of cookies.
Burned his thighs with her cigarette
when he dribbled pee on the bathroom floor.
Then, over time, this boyfriend and that
crawled from her bed, and took turns
getting him drunk or high,
fondling him, calling him *faggot*.
When he reached fifteen he said he couldn't feel a thing.
Didn't give a damn, either.
The kitchen crew say
for a while he posed as a bodybuilder.
Now he wears mascara, glittery nail polish,
pulls his hair into a lank ponytail.
Even on this warm spring morning,
he drapes his frame in an ankle-length winter coat,
off the shoulder, like a 1940's movie star.
Every day he shows up at the soup kitchen, they say,
standing at the Dutch door asking for Sister
who comes out of her office with travel-size tubes
of toothpaste, mouthwash, and a comb.
She folds his fingers around a bar of soap
for the brittle body he hasn't washed in god-knows-how-long.
I watch how she listens to him with her eyes and mouth,
how her face says *You are always welcome here,*
how the two of them hold the many shards of his life
he's brought her in a plastic garbage bag.
Maybe her life, too,

spreading all of it on a table,
lacquering the pieces together,
making the seams shine with
something like gold.

Shipbreaking

(for Nagui)

Other dawns we'd steam smoothly into port,
  gliding together out of the gulf of night,
    oblivious to the deep brain's navigation

  through sleep, its autonomic governance
of our temperature-controlled flesh,
blood pressure, the gut's peristalsis, breath.

Now, in this late year and a deeper gulf,
  our hearts hammer against the inner ear,
        lungs in their pleura scrape the ribs.

        Knees like cold gears grind.

I want more voyaging time, you say. I say the same.
  But the dry dock age arrives,
    when repairs can't forestall the scuttle

  starting soon enough, long or short.
  Already these once-young hulls have begun
the rattle and the ratcheting down

of winches and whining pulleys. What remains
  of bodies rusts into red nothingness,
        rudder, keel, and spar.

Available Light

(Leesburg Stockade, GA, 1963)

Does he ask them?
Does he shout, *Look this way!*
when he raises the light meter and rolls
the lens between thumb and forefinger
to focus on the little knot of prisoners?

Girls incarcerated and scared,
summoned from their hushed huddle in a cinder block cell
by the photographer at the back of that stark space.
They stand at a window barred with iron
like teeth of a mouth clamped shut.

Girls in shorts, pedal-pushers, a kente-patterned
sheath, a straight skirt, all skinny-legged and shod
in cheap canvas and flip-flops, confined
in the chiaroscuro of America's chronic rage.

The shutter is slow and the film
is silvered enough to save available light
cradling the dark of these faces in a Georgia jail,
black and white proof of the grit
of this one righteous girl and that,
uncowed by cops or cameras, defiant
arms on narrow hips, hands shoved into pockets,
nudging a fugitive sprig of hair under a scarf.

And the littlest one,
sitting on the concrete floor, flattening
her back against a wall, eyeing the photographer—

Maybe she's tired, thinking of home,
her worried mama on her mind.
Maybe she's thinking of nothing at all.
Maybe she's fixing to form words
her foremothers did not dare: *Mister?*
What are you looking at?

The Mule

(after Ellen Bryant Voigt, with a line from William Faulkner)

A man kills a mule with a hammer or a two-by-four.
No one is really sure. A poet writes this

about her father's father. It is a bob-end
of a family tale only a few of her kin remember.

He was a wonder of indecipherable silence,
this young farmer from a prior age.

The reader is meant to consider this man
plowing his field,

the sweat and lather of the work,
the futile confrontation with weariness.

It's hard to know if the poet mourns him—
she does not romanticize.

But the poem makes me think of the mule
hoof-deep and halt in the riven ground,

welts the man's leather lash has made livid
on belly and flank weeping with serum and pain,
            the bludgeon retrieved from the barn.

Perhaps the mule resigned itself to the fate
of dumb resistance to the prod.

They are intelligent beings, after all.
Smarter than horses, some say.

The mule no doubt knew that pulling the yoke
one more inch would have exceeded a boundary.

Such is the mule, muscled with self-knowledge,
wiser than Aristotle.

It cannot be untrue to itself.
Unlike a man who wields a plank
      and pounds mule blood into the earth.

How Much Farther Does the Arc Have to Bend?

Take, for example, the Michigan boy,
all of fourteen, who doesn't look his
age and has never committed a crime.

The newspaper says he missed the school bus
taking him across town. Says that his mother
took his cell phone (whatever was the reason,

the paper doesn't say), so he couldn't call. Still,
he wants to go to class. He begins to walk the distance
between the bus stop and his school in a far suburb.

The paper says after a while he lost his way in the cat's
cradle of turns between his house and Rochester Hills.
It was past dawn, and the suburban street was empty.

Maybe he sees a reclusive tabby yawning on a
windowsill. Maybe he hears a garage door whine
on its track. Maybe he watches a car whirr down the street,

then turn into an alley. After the engine sounds fade,
all that remains is the quiet blue chill of early
spring curling around his ankles.

You'd think he'd panic, that fear would ripple through his
chest like a jazz riff. But the boy has faith in the world,
in its ineffable order, since he knows his mother loves him.

Loves him enough to separate him from whoever was on
the other end of that cell phone and *god-knows-what-else.*
The boy carries that faith up the front steps of a

house with a porch, and a sign that says *Please ring,*
a faith that from this house someone kind, (maybe
someone like his mother) might open the door, show him the way.

A woman comes to the buzzing bell (let's say she
pulls a sheer curtain panel from the sidelight), and lands
her eye on the lanky boy with large glasses, standing back,

staring calmly at the door, waiting. The paper says
he was already forming the words, *Good morning, ma'am,*
when he hears the woman scream.

Then a man comes (let's say he, too, stares through the sidelight),
cracks open the door and lifts a shotgun to the boy's head.
What choice does the boy have but to turn and sprint down the

steps as the barrel blast sizzles past his ear? The paper says
the county sheriff arrested the man for attempted murder.
But the man has a story he will tell the newspaper reporter,

the lie and justification he'll give about the shiftless
and the larcenous, the homicidal and criminally insane,
addicted predators everybody knows breed (he says) in the bowels

of America's cities like the parasites they are, and now, *this boy*
who looks older than fourteen (he says), and who in early
morning emerges from that same unfathomable blackness

to land at his front door. The man says he could not rein in his fear.
Just like the cop in Carolina a few years back, who, after he
shot a man in cold blood on the side of a road, said to himself,

They will believe whatever I tell them, because I am the law,
and I am white.

The paper calls out the aggression and the lie.
But the boy and his mother have no more peace
than the ancestors who fled Alabama and Georgia.

Because history is supposed to bend toward justice.
Because it's been too long, and America won't stop asking,
What the hell are they doing in our neighborhoods?

Father

Was it the infant you cradled in your arms,
the milky breath of her baby hair?
Was it her feathered eyelashes
her closed eyes rocking like little boats in the sea of sleep?
Was it her fingertips you kissed as she slept,
the flickering smile as she dreamed?
Was it her fevers and fluxes in the middle of the night?
Was it the bedtime stories,
the songs you sang in the car?
Was it her toothless giggle at your daddy jokes,
the first day of school, the kindergarten graduation?
Was it the fact you could not save your child
                    that made you remember and remember and remember?

Each memory a torment, each a lash against the heart.
And surely you could not foresee that December day,
the mute adolescent anger, the rage and the rifle of a boy's
stalking darkness, against which you could give no safety.

Even the President wept.

Was it *all* of that, father? And the torpor of the nation
the shameless torpor of us, with the rants of squalid men
which caused your world to fall finally and forever from its axis
and made grief take you down into its cave
to crush you?

Notes for a Poem on West 37th

(What you see)

He's working three breakfast orders, the cook, his aboriginal head diademed with sweat, hands darting like Yucatán parakeets.

(What you suspect he had to do; what he now is doing)

He got up at four this morning, took the subway out of Brooklyn, made it into Manhattan by five. At six, he's ladling grease onto hot cast iron, pouring what will become your Denver omelet from a stainless-steel bowl.

(What you figure is going on at this very moment)

His wife is still asleep. She got home at midnight from her janitorial shift on Wall Street. The twelve-year old shakes the little ones out of bed, makes sure they brush their teeth, pours them Cheerios, walks them to school.

(What you imagine will happen)

Their father will be back by four this afternoon. Their mother will be out again, on the J train. They'll do this six, maybe seven days a week. You figure most of what they make goes into rent. Then, food and train fare, the kids' coats and boots. Maybe a little something for a sister-in-law back home.

(Because you know this story)

The cook folds in the onions and cheese. He has hands like your father, who arrived in this country with an uncle and two cousins, speaking only Spanish. All his life he did this kind of work. When you came along, he bought you shoes, made you *café con leche*, laying it out on the table with *pan y mantequilla* before it was time for school. On those mornings, how your love for him streamed *como un aguacero*, a tropical downpour of a child's adoration.

Dawn in a Hotel Room in a Large City

Through the dark the sun comes to the tall bay windows
where I turn east, south, west.

Lights along the streets river red and gold.
In the gloaming, the white moon glides west.

Out of bedrock, water climbs two hundred feet,
and enters the tap on the shower wall.

It falls through my hair and hands,
falls on my shoulders and breasts.

I give my face to it.
I turn and turn in the warmth.

And it goes back to the earth,
taking whatever of me I have washed away.

Father,

my body has made use of yesterday's food.
I want to tell you I thanked each thing that gave its life

so I could write these words. It was dawn then, too, when
I sat with you, your face burning with light.

Tell me what you saw
when you looked on your city from a height like this.

I'm listening.
I'm still a small child on the way to school.

This World Holding On

(after Lucie Brock-Broido, in memoriam)

I

But you are no longer
in the dominion of your body.
Gone into the fire
are your Rapunzel hair
and the dark winter cap
rimmed with fur.

Who will wear your crown now?

I knew you only
in the bravura of your lines, the wildness of them.
I don't see, don't sing like you.
But I'm voicing you onto this page.

I send you into a spring born of new rain.
Welcome to this meadow.

II

Who has not asked herself,
What has shaped you? Where are you from?

I say George Bellows and Edward Hopper.
I say steam engines on the Pennsy line.
Dieseled. Electrified. Devised to snake through
the subaqueous gut of the Hudson and East Rivers,
Manhattan's silt and adamant.

I say Holland and Lincoln tunnels,
and McKim's homage to Rome
before the City of New York and the Pennsylvania Railroad

made it a pit of plastic and broken glass.
Then they tore it down.

I say slagged coal slung and stoked into fireboxes burning.
Black stacks, steel-gray plumes staining the January sky.

I say an uncle dispatched too young into the frozen earth,
his sister Margie slumped at the phone.
And on the way to the funeral Mass,
my white sleeves sooted, elbow to wrist,
on the open-windowed ledge of the train car.
her slap on the side of my face when she sees this.

Trains carried our weeping.

III

Beyond the blackness of tunnels an electric city lay.

                                   And I,
daughter of a Bronx plumber's daughter,
the cause for novenas to Our Lady of Perpetual Help
in the parish of her Immaculate Conception, stood
under the el tracks, my hand in Margie's hand,
feeling fingers of light fan over us like an anointing.

                                  But dawn
in the world's capital was a dirty sun prismed down
through el ties creosoted and nailed to rails
over a liver-colored street in Sunnyside, Queens.
                                   And the sun
hid from Harlem and the Bronx, borough of my birth,
hid from the palisades of the Hudson River and New Jersey,
hid from Pittsburgh, Appalachian city of your birth.

                              Who murdered this star
in the coke-gray float of exhausted hydrocarbons?

IV

Poet, you and I are
children of the same mistral escarpments
of iron and fossilized conifers,
                  we were birthed
into the same the refinery-cracked maelstrom and muck
of Industrial America, parent of robber barons, ruler of the world.

You said you wanted
              One thing. One thing. One thing.
You hungered (you said) for life after this life.
Now, this is something I've heard tell of.

Then let me chant what I hear spoken
into the ear of the wind:

     Everything you are, I am—

Malignant breasts and scarred lungs,
hearts stopped in mid-beat, teratogenic
ovaries, prolapsed wombs, wandering wall eyes,
teeth that never descended but remained failed buds in the gum,
swollen knees, squamous growths and melanomas,
frantic minds vibrating in insomniac bodies,
ladders of arthritic bones—

              you are
                    the flowers I love into bloom
                    in the vast field of being.

Even now. Even now. Even now,
we are standing in the garden of all things.

Laudate Omnes

(for Asher, young grandson)

Let's talk
to the bees.

       Let's say,

Ladies, thank you
each and all

for coming this day
to the hyssop and bergamot.

Thank you
for diving

into the boggy throats
of pale blue sage.

Thank you
for letting sticky

pollen crawl
up your hairy legs.

Thank you
for the sweet spit of the hive.

Now to the trees turn and say,
Brothers,

I don't know all your names
or what families you belong to,

but you over there,
tall and handsome with your spiky green:

if you and I were lone survivors
of a meteorological catastrophe,

I'd live with you.
I'd hole up under your branches.

Leaves and rain
would be our food and drink each day.

Now let's say thanks and thanks and thanks
for the hive's honeyed paradise,

for meadows of thick-maned mares
drowsing with their foals,

for bees, horses, and trees,
oceans, plains, and the sky,

Let's say thanks
for the darkness between stars

which is not an emptiness,
but a rookery

where God dreams us.
And if we found ourselves

on a comet flying
beyond Pluto's orbit,

even there we would
be not separate and alone,

but we would be
as now we are

in the heart of things,
the very heart.

Mother and Daughter, Two Voices

III.

Daughter

Be happy for me in my seventieth year,
for landing on this branch higher than you were fated to reach.

Your wings broke too soon,
your chronic storms bent too hard those necessary bones.
Though in the staggered ascent through my own sky
you taught me something of true flight.

I saw you move toward me in a dream, your face and lips.
I heard you speak as on that first day without you.
Each word a musical note, each phrase a percussive beat,
You must go on.

I hear you now.
In the car,
as I swoop and bank
down a Carolina highway, music throbbing,
timbal, clave, and *batá* singing, *Live! Live!*

Notes

"Woman on a Plane," p. 15, after Goli Taragui, "A House in Heaven," short story.

"Annunciation," p. 33, after Lynn Emmanuel's "Stone Soup."

"What the Midwife Said," p. 35. To Coral Edith O'Brien (1921-2008), *in memoriam.*

"To My Not Baby," p. 37, after Lucille Clifton's "the lost baby poem."

"Neighbors," p, 43. This partly ekphrastic sequence details a painting by William Robilliard, brother of Margaret (Margie) García (née, Robilliard) ca. 1956-58.

"What Margie Wrote *in memoriam* about Her Brother," p. 49, poem by Margaret M. Robilliard in her own hand on August 3, 1965.

"Margie's Daughter Talks Back," p. 50, originally published as "It's OK to Say These Things," in *Red Sky*, 2016. See also, Lucie Brock Broido, "After the Grand Perhaps," in *A Hunger.*

"Dreaming of My Father," p. 56, after Lucille Clifton, "forgiving my father."

"Available Light," p. 63, on a photograph by Danny Lyon, in *Reflections: Yale Divinity School Magazine of Theological and Ethical Inquiry,* Fall, 2016, p.50.

"The Mule," p. 64, after Ellen Bryant Voigt, "Short Story"; "bob-end tale" comes from William Faulkner, *Absalom! Absalom!*

"How Much Farther Does the Arc Have to Bend?" p 66, has its basis in the 2018 news story of a young boy in Michigan.

"Father," p. 68, references the death of Jeremy Richman, father of Avielle Richman who was murdered along with twenty-six others at Sandyhook Elementary School in Newtown, CT, in December 2012.

"This World Holding On," p. 71, after Lucie Brock-Broido, *in memoriam*. Also, Walt Whitman and Adonis (Ali Ahmad Saïd). Poems by Lucy Brock-Broido cited or referenced include "When the God Go, Half-Gods Arrive," *The Master Letters;* "The One Theme of Which Everything Else is a Variation," *Trouble in Mind;* "A Meadow," *Stay, Illusion* "After the Grand Perhaps," *A Hunger.*

Acknowledgments

I am grateful to the editors of the following print and electronic journals for accepting a number of poems in *All the Way to China:*

Old Mountain Press: "Gray-Eyed Bronx Girl," "My Not-Baby, "Blue Vase
    With Dark Foliage."
Willawaw Journal, "Heading West," "First Memory," "Purification,"
    "Annunciation."
2019 Nazim Hikmet, proceedings: "My Dead, You Cannot Visit Them,"
    "Marianne," "Kintsugi."
Peacock Journal: "Portrait of My Cuban Father," "Dawn in a Hotel Room."
Negative Capability: "In the Faded Photo, My Toddler Self at the Bronx
    Zoo" published as "Memory Trace."
Red Sky, Sable Press: "Margie's Daughter Talks Back," (previous title, "It's
    OK to Say These Things".
Presence: "Dreaming of My Father."
3Elements Review: "How Much Farther Does the Arc Have to Bend."
Image: "The Mule."
Survive and Thrive (medical journal of the University of St Cloud, MN):
    "Father."

The following poems received Pushcart Prize nominations:

"Kintsugi" (also, 2nd prize, 2019 Nazim Hikmet International poetry
    competition)
"Maryanne" (also, 2nd prize, 2019 Nazim Hikmet International poetry
    competition)
"My Dead, You Cannot Visit Them" (also, 2nd prize, 2019 Nazim Hikmet
    International poetry competition)
"How Much Farther Does the Arc Have to Bend (*3Elements*)

Other Awards and Recognitions:

"Memory Trace," *Negative Capability* "Featured Poet" section, 2015.
"Annunciation," Finalist, Poet Laureate Contest, North Carolina Poetry
    Society, 2018
"Laudate Omnes," Finalist, Randall Jarrell competition, North Carolina
    Writers Network, 2019.

"Margie Takes a Courageous Stand," Finalist, Randall Jarrell competition, North Carolina Writers Network, 2020.
"My Not Baby," Finalist, Randall Jarrell competition, North Carolina Writers Network, 2020.
"Margie Skips a Grade," Finalist, Poet Laureate Contest, North Carolina Poetry Society, 2020.

Maria Rouphail, PhD, is Senior Lecturer Emerita from North Carolina State University, where she taught courses in World Literature and where she also served as an academic adviser to the English major. She is Poetry Editor of *Main Street Rag*. She has published two collections: *Apertures* (Finishing Line Press, New Women's Voices) and *Second Skin* (Main Street Rag). Her third collection, *All the Way to China*, was a 2020 finalist in both the University of Wisconsin Brittingham Poetry and the Blue Light Press competitions. A five-time Pushcart nominee, she lives in Raleigh.